Cover design by Mark Labbe'. Design Contributors: Kendall
Thorsell, Jeremy Dorlon, and Juan Garnica.

Printed in the United States of America.

ISBN: 9780989073516

LOVE, IN ITS' PURITY

DEDICATION

This book is dedicated to my youngest son, Michael. Because of your insatiable quest for knowledge, you inspire me to seek the answers. I love you.

Ron Jr. and Jason, who accepted Michael into their family and their hearts, thank you. I love you guys.

Ron, my husband, you always believed in me. This book is just as much a victory for you, as it is for me. I will always love you.

ACKNOWLEDGMENTS

Without the love, prayers, and help from the following people this book would not exist: Barbara Weiss, Marcia Thorsell, Ruthanne Dorlon; John and Cheryl Litton, Carol Leff, Andrea Bennett, Ezekiel and Monica Brooks.

"Thank you" to the six couples who shared their experiences and deep convictions of faith and redemption: Rob and Vangie, Bill and Jenny, Briggs and Kara, Jeff and Crystal, Jamey and Jeannie, John and Christa.

TABLE OF CONTENTS

INTRODUCTION

Is it possible to be in love and remain sexually pure before marriage? The answer is "Yes!"

Love, In Its Purity is not your typical book. It is in a question and answer format. This book was developed to answer questions like, "How do I remain sexually pure? What happens if I have sex before marriage? Is there hope? Will God still love me?

You don't have to be sexually impure. You don't have to remain sexually impure. There is hope in God.

The following text was taken from recorded questions and answers of six couples. The text is edited to make their answers more clear.

I pray you find this book simple, clear, and powerful.

ROB and VANGIE

How did you meet?

Rob: I was at a church camp when I met Vangie. I saw certain qualities in her that I hadn't found in anyone else. That was when I realized, man, this is the girl.

I have a very strong opinion. When you say, "I love you" to someone from a romantic standpoint, it means, "I am committed to you." The next words you should be prepared to say are, "Will you marry me?" On our first official date I told Vangie I loved her.

Vangie: I was introduced to Rob at a Christian Middle School where he led worship at my friends youth group. I didn't date many men. If I didn't think he was a man of God and I could marry him tomorrow, forget it.

I wanted to marry a man like my dad, light hair, and kind of calm. Rob is the exact opposite. He has dark hair. He is Italian, loud, and likes to talk, a life of the party type of person. Yet, Rob really loves the Lord. I fell in love with him.

Who influenced you the most?

Rob: I had the most phenomenal youth pastor. He was open, and very honest.

He always challenged us to protect our virginity. He said, "The tendency in many youth is when they realize there is an attraction, or they realize they are struggling with lust, or something of that nature…is to go to the altar, weep, and say, "God take away this desire."

My youth pastor said, "If God takes that desire away you are going to have a lot of problems. If you are not physically attracted to the opposite sex, then, (a) there's something wrong with you, or (b) you are with the wrong person. If you are with someone you genuinely love and care about, there will be a very strong physical attraction."

Vangie: My parents love for me, and their teaching the Word of God had the most impact on me. I never felt like I needed to search for love. My dad would also ask me, "Are you saving yourself?" As a little girl my mother always said, "Vangie, don't throw away your kisses like candy." I knew my virginity was something special that was to be given only to my husband.

Why do you remain sexually pure?

Rob: My parents were divorced, and I had all the markings in my home of absolute moral failure. Given that scenario, a high school counselor told me if I "Amounted to anything, it would be an incredible shock to her."

I certainly had every opportunity to be immoral. I had a mom that worked. I could have brought girls home after school. But, deep inside my heart I knew that I did not want to give away my virginity. That was saved for "The one!" I am very attracted to Vangie. And, yes, it can be very difficult. I am a normal man. Pastor Alex

Clattenburg told me, "You are a pastor, but you are a man first."

Vangie and I had opportunities where premarital sex could have happened. However, I almost see it as injuring her. Vangie and I have come into a covenant together that this is of utmost importance to us. We have a deep respect for each other. I have the utmost respect for Vangie. I would never, and could never, imagine taking advantage of her.

Our remaining sexually pure before marriage is going to be one of the greatest celebrations, and probably one of the greatest victories in my life. I can cross the finish line, and say, "Yeah, I did this! And, I did it right!"

Vangie: I knew I was loved by my mom and dad. I knew my virginity was something special. I had girlfriends in school who were crying because they let boys touch them sexually.

Some girls didn't have a loving father in their lives. They were either promiscuous, or did not have self-respect for themselves. They always had to have a boyfriend to make them feel loved. I didn't need a boyfriend to make me feel loved.

I've been in situations where I had a choice to make. To me, any advance made toward me was totally refused. I wanted to save myself for my husband. I chose to do it God's way. Not doing it God's way causes heartache.

What do you say to the person who has lost their virginity?

Rob: I tell people the moment you are saved your sins are washed away. God looks at a pure person, someone that is a new creation. Their past is never remembered by God.

Vangie: When people get saved, they have to deal with the same situations after they are saved, that they had to deal with before they were saved. Salvation it's a new way of handling things. The best thing we can do is have grace for them, to come at them with open arms, and to love them. Let them know Jesus died for them, and cleanses them from all unrighteousness. God will help them.

Do you have any last words?

Rob and Vangie: The moment you are saved, your sins are washed away. "Old things are passed away, behold, all things are made new." (2 Corinthians 5:17)

You are a new creation spiritually, and internally you are a virgin. Physically and emotionally you may not be, but spiritually you are. When God looks at you, God looks at a pure person."

BILL and JENNY

How did you meet?

Bill: I met Jenny at a church in Illinois. I was working as a pastoral intern at the church with the college and career students. Jenny attended the life group I led.

Jenny: I was about sixteen years old when I saw Bill out of thousands of people at a Carmen Concert. After the concert I was walking up the steps and I saw Bill again. He was talking with some girls. In my heart I thought "This is one guy that would never date me because I don't have something he requires in a girl." I didn't know that "something" was Jesus Christ. But, I knew he was off limits.

When I graduated from high school my boyfriend and I visited a church. I joined a new believers' class being taught by a woman named, Karen. Karen talked about her son who was a pastoral intern at the church. Since all the pastors were older, I assumed he was in his forties with a balding head.

One day I met Karen at the church office. I saw a picture on her desk. She said, "This is my son who works here, and he's a pastor." I remembered he was the same guy I saw at the Carmen Concert years before. I was simply amazed me how God did that.

Who influenced you the most?

Bill: My mother was very active in helping me. Although I made some bad choices, I always knew I was going to have to come home and face my mother.

The other person that helped me was my youth pastor. He would say, "If you are sitting on a sofa, you need to sit on a sofa, and not lay down next to each other."

He would talk about how to sit on a sofa (couch), and "not getting into a comfortable, cozy position (especially close to another person), because one thing leads to another." By having a youth pastor who would talk honestly, and give practical tips on how to avoid certain things was definitely beneficial and helpful in my own life.

Spiritually, when I was in the Word of God, I was doing well. The Bible says, "Keep yourself pure." (I Timothy 5: 22) How does a man keep himself pure? It is by staying in the Word of God. The Word of God has a lot to do with helping you to stay pure; although, at that stage of the game it seems like you walk on ice. For me, the more I could avoid temptation, the easier it was not to fall into temptation.

Jenny: God, my husband, and my mother-in-law have influenced me the most. Bill and I have grown together in the Lord. I see him so much as my husband, obviously, but also my spiritual leader.

Why did you remain sexually pure?

Bill: Sexual purity was a conviction we both had. One of the greatest struggles I had in remaining pure was just the time spent in dating.

14

My experience in dating was, time equals intimacy. The more time you spent together, the more intimate you naturally became. I found myself in several dating relationships where the natural progression was to get as physically involved, as I was emotionally involved.

For me, dating became a difficult challenge that I faced in remaining sexually pure. Not in terms of intercourse only, but in keeping my thoughts pure. However, regardless of how much I prayed and read the Bible, if I continued to subject myself to certain temptations, it was just a matter of time before I found myself falling into those temptations.

The greatest decision you can make to safeguard yourself is to avoid all opportunities for sin. Someone once told me "The strongest man is a man who knows his weakness and runs from it."

I made a decision not to date anyone for two years. After the two year period, I dated a young lady. She was not the right person for me.

Jenny was somebody I felt close to, and wanted to marry.

Jenny: I didn't know about being sexually pure, except for my conscience, until I was taught the Word of God. It was a struggle for us, even with him being in the ministry, because I didn't make it easy for him. I came from the world, and my clothes were of the world.

We decided to remain sexually pure because it was biblical, and for Bill. We were presenting ourselves to each other, but more importantly to God.

What do you say to the person who has lost their virginity?

Bill: I believe God is a God of restoration. I believe we serve a God of a second chance. I believe it is never too late to make a stand to be sexually pure, and to walk in holiness. In spite of your past, when you make a decision to walk it out right, God honors that choice.

Jenny: I would like to speak to the youth who have lost their virginity, and to the ones who didn't go all the way, but you've messed up. Repent! Just start again!

I totally believe there is such a thing as being a "spiritually rebuilt virgin." God says He "makes us a new creation" (2 Corinthians 5:17).

Yet, at the same time new creatures still have old memories. You have to deal with those memories. You have to constantly be on guard.

If you know something is going to tempt you, stay away from it. Just like an alcoholic stays away from the bottle, you stay away from something that is going to tempt you. If you know a certain person has lust on their mind, and you are attracted to that person, stay away from them. If something is wrong in your heart when you are around somebody, and you just feel yucky (disgusting or unpleasant), stay away from them! Pray for people that walk in impurity, but stay away from them for your own sake.

I believe young people can remain sexually pure. *It is not unattainable*. Don't give into the old lie that your past is your future, because it's not! When you accept Jesus Christ as your Savior, your past is gone. It is erased in God's eyes.

Get in the Word of God, and around friends who have chosen to remain sexually pure for their future husband or wife. Concentrate on the future. Whether you have stayed a virgin, or whether you have walked in the lifestyle of the impure, you just need to go forth in Christ.

Do you have any last words?

Bill: If I could do it all over again, I would avoid dating one specific person. I would enjoy the presence of having a lot of girl friends that I was not emotionally or physically attached to.

I found characteristics and qualities in each girl I liked who had been a part of my life. It was a way to find out what I really wanted in a wife, without falling into sin. Be a part of a healthy group dating scenario where you are always with other people.

Jenny: People need to know they are special. No matter what your background is, God is able to clean it up. God can make a good thing out of a bad thing. You can remain sexually pure and save yourself for your future spouse. When you walk with God, He brings the right mate for you.

"Trust in the Lord with all your heart and lean not on your own understanding." (Proverbs 3:5, 6)

JAMIE and JEANNIE

How did you meet?

We met at Rama Bible College in Tulsa,
Oklahoma.

Who influenced you the most?

Jamey: My parents influenced me the most by
teaching me the Word of God.

Jeannie: I would have to say my mother
influenced me the most. She helped me stay
strong spiritually and physically. She knew
whenever I wasn't in the Word of God. She
would say, "Jeannie, you must be in the Word.
You must get yourself back in the Word." My
mom was always like a check and balance
system for me. She was always encouraging me
in the Lord.

Why did you remain sexually pure?

Jamey: My parents taught me about morality.
They also taught me about abstaining from

20

premarital sex. It was very important in God's standards, and in God's way of doing things here on the earth.

Jeannie: I knew it was a gift I could only give to one person. I wanted it to be with the man I would be with for the rest of my life. I made the choice to wait. Not only because of what God said, but because I didn't want the heartache of giving myself to a man, and then not having him by my side and be a covenant partner in marriage. I wanted it to be a gift I could give to my husband.

What do you say to the person who has lost their virginity?

Jamey and Jeannie: If you have already entered into sexual satisfaction before marriage, you must ask God to forgive you of your sin (because it is sin).

The Bible also says, "As far as the East is from the West, so far has He removed our transgressions from us." (Psalm 103:12)

21

You must have an understanding of who our Heavenly Father is. In our natural mind we can't comprehend how He can forgive and forget our sins. God loves you with an unconditional love.

Once you receive Jesus in your heart and life, you begin to understand His love. His love for you endures forever. It is His love that covers a multitude of sins. It is His love that cleanses you.

We want to say, "Be encouraged!" The battlefield is in your mind. Don't allow the devil to defeat you in your mind. You have to get in the Word of God, and renew your mind. Get around other people that are of like faith, that believe the same thing you believe.

If being sexually pure is a struggle in your life, you must have accountability. If it's not a struggle, you still need to be around people who are abstaining from sex until marriage.

Do you have any last words?

Jamey and Jeannie: We would like to say, "It is God's will for you to remain sexually pure." You can remain sexually pure! You have to see yourself, through faith in God, that you can be victorious.

The Bible says, "We are more than conquerors through Him (Jesus Christ) who loved us." (Romans 8:37)

In other words, you can change the world around you, rather than the world changing you. God loves you, no matter what you have done in the past. See yourself as winners...not losers. You might not have had a father or mother who built you up or encouraged you. But, you have a Heavenly Father who loves you with an everlasting love."

BRIGGS and KARA

How did you meet?

Briggs and Kara: We met at a college-age Bible study at church. We were friends about a year before we started dating.

Who influenced you the most?

Briggs: I guess it would be my mom. I used to be with both my mom and dad until they divorced.

Kara: My parents influenced me the most. I grew up surrounded by other believers. The principles of being sexually pure before marriage were instilled in me when I was younger, and carried through to my teenage years.

One thing that helped me was Briggs and I talking it over at the beginning of our relationship. When the other person wants to remain sexually pure before marriage just as you do, then it is a lot easier. There is no pressure.

When I struggled with, you know, with lust or whatever, Briggs helped me in that area.

Why do you remain sexually pure?

Briggs and Kara: We have chosen to remain sexually pure before marriage. Throughout the Bible and through the scriptures God has laid out the plan for marriage. We are to remain sexually pure before (and after) marriage.

Most of the time people base their relationships on sexual and physical things. But doing it God's way, without getting so physical, you can learn a lot about that person. You get the opportunity to know them better. It is not so focused on the physical only.

What do you say to the person who has lost their virginity?

Briggs: The first thing you need to know is who God is, how much He loves you, and what He's done for you. You need to know that marriage was designed by God. It's only going to work if you follow His way.

Kara: First, I would make it clear that God has forgiven you. In fact, He doesn't even remember it anymore. But, from now on the same Biblical principles apply. I encourage you, especially if you are a new believer, to find Christian friends who won't bring you down.

Even we struggled a little by kissing right away and stuff like that. The biggest thing that helps is not to put yourself in a position where you may be tempted to do the wrong thing.

If you are alone in your parents' house, you know, that is a big temptation. Once you start kissing and doing other things, it just progresses further and further.

If you plan from the beginning not to even do those things, it makes it a lot easier to remain sexually pure.

Do you have any last words?

Briggs: The man is the spiritual leader in a relationship. I believe the responsibility lies more on the man (it does rely some on the woman). You need to stop and think about who has to be the strong one, and don't give into the stupid temptations.

I have found the best thing is to agree with God that sex outside of marriage is wrong. Ask God for strength to get out of that temptation.

At Bible College we had to take a class on family. Both of us recommend you read *The Marriage Builder* by Larry Crabb. It says, "If you really want to have a good relationship, you need to have spiritual oneness together. Once you have spiritual oneness, you can have soul oneness. Once you have soul oneness together, after marriage, you can have a blessed physical oneness."

Kara: 2 Timothy 2:22 says, "To flee youthful lusts." I mean, it is very hard. The easiest thing to do is just leave and get out of the situation, and out of the temptation.

It is important to have your own devotional time, your quiet time with the Lord.

It is also important to have a quiet time of reading the Bible, and praying with your significant other. Studying the Bible on different scriptures that talk about sexual immorality and sexual purity helps you to stay strong.

When you are brought together spiritually, it helps everything else fall into place. I don't know why, but in our relationship it just helps."

JOHN and CHRISTA

How did you meet?

John and Christa: "Christa and I met at a church summer camp. After high school Christa moved to Florida. After college, I moved back home to Florida. We were already good friends. However, somewhere in there it shifted and we started to date, and many moons later we got married.

Who influenced you the most?

John and Christa: Our parents, pastors, and football coaches.

Why did you remain sexually pure?

John: First of all we decided to remain pure because that's what the Bible says, and it is what we were taught growing up. I had been taught there is a spiritual connection, as well as a physical connection.

My first kiss was with my wife. I felt like a
million dollars! You have to understand that
with the first kiss there is a high that comes.
Like drugs, people are trying to get that first
high. They go to stronger drugs in order to get to
that same level.

In the same way, that is what happens when you
have your first kiss. When you continue with
your relationship, the kiss looses that passion,
that high. So, you go a little bit further the next
time.

Christa and I knew sexual purity was a standard
God had set. We decided to keep that standard
because we wanted to honor God. It says in the
Word of God to "Keep yourself pure." (I Timothy
5:22)

The way you keep yourself pure is to set your
standards before you start in a relationship.
Both of you have to agree on those standards.

The Bible says in 2 Corinthians 6:14, "don't be
…unequally yoked." Most people believe it is

between a sinner and a saint, or a person who is saved or unsaved, and it is.

It is also between a person who is committed to the Lord, or lukewarm. There is just as big a gap between a person who is committed to the Lord and a person who is lukewarm, as there is between the saved and the unsaved. If you have two different standards, neither of you will hit the target.

Christa: We decided we were going to remain pure, and because it talks about it in the Bible.

I look at it this way - you can have three wrapped presents to open. One present can be perfectly wrapped with nothing torn. The second present might be torn a little bit on the edge. The third present is all messed up. It doesn't even have a bow on it anymore, and most of the wrapping paper is torn off.

Of course, when you look at the three presents, you are going to want the one not touched yet. For me, that is what I got in my husband, John. John had never kissed, nor hugged girls in a

31

sexual way. He never told a girl he loved her, and he never held hands with girls or anything like that. I got the perfect package.

But for me, I couldn't say that. I was more like the second present. I was a little bit torn on the inside. I had already dated, and I was scarred from those relationships.

What do you say to the person who has lost their virginity?

John and Christa: God still loves them, and He can restore them. They can make a commitment to lead a pure life to honor God from that point on.

If you want more information on why you should keep yourself pure, check out the book *The Seven Checkpoints* by Andy Stanley and Stuart Hall. Checkpoint number three is one of the best passages on maintaining a pure life we've ever read.

Once you hold someone's hand, give those hugs, or do any sexual thing with that person, you cannot take it back. You cannot look at that person the same way ever again. It changes your entire relationship. There is a "soul tie" that has taken place, a "tying" of your heart to that person.

If you've had times where you messed up with other people, you have to ask God to break those "soul ties" and make you pure again. God is the great physician! He can heal broken hearts, He can mend wounds.

Do you have any last words?

John: Yes! When I was around ten years old, I heard a teaching on soul ties. A "soul tie" is something you have with a person. Anytime you kiss someone, you have a soul tie.

Genesis 2:24 says, "…and they shall be one flesh." There is a "tie" in intimacy between a man and a woman. They truly do become one in spirit, soul, and body.

Christa: The best thing about God is that He forgives, and forgets our sins. The second thing is that He and the Holy Spirit can always make you pure again.

If you've already lost everything in a relationship as far as your virginity is concerned, God can restore you. God can give it back, just like it was your first time.

I know, because I was raped in a relationship. My first experience with any of that kind of stuff was an awful one. God restored everything back, and gave me something ten times better, my husband, John."

JEFF and CRYSTAL

How did you meet?

Jeff: "We met in the Rehab Room at Warner Southern College.

Crystal: As Jeff said, we met in the Rehabilitation room at Warner Southern College. We were both injured at the same time.

Who influenced you the most?

Jeff: My father. He taught me so much about responsibility, and about taking care of things. He taught me about letting your "Yes"… be… "Yes,"and your "No" …be… "No."

Crystal: I would say my mother. My mom always prayed, and she made sure everything was done in our life. I knew my dad loved me also. He would ask, "Crystal, are you saving yourself for marriage?"

Why did you remain sexually pure?

Jeff: I was a non-Christian growing up. My answer is different. I had sex with several women. It was something that was like a drug to me. It was like an addiction.

Alcohol was not an addiction, but sex was. It really had a stronghold on me. I was into everything you could think of, pornography, clubs, even strip clubs and things like that. I was on the far end of being immoral.

When I met Crystal there was something different, something unique about her. I didn't want to do anything sexually impure with her. With the other women, there was nothing unique about them. I knew what they wanted.

But, Crystal was something totally different. There was a treasure deep within her that I wanted to find.

Crystal: Jeff and I had struggles just like anyone else. I knew this was the man I was going to marry. Jeff was a one hundred percent gentleman. We knew we wanted something special on our honeymoon. We helped each other. Also, our church leaders helped us. They spoke into our lives the Word of God, and gave us advice on how to stay pure before marriage.

What do you say to the person who has lost their virginity?

Jeff: Well, I would be speaking of myself. I lost my virginity when I was 14 years old with a girl I really didn't even know. It just happened. It was something that was done and over within five minutes. Even before the age of 14, I had seen pornographic magazines and things like that, which led to the sexual impurity.

If I could, I would do anything to take my virginity back. But thank God, through Jesus Christ, I have forgiveness. Before I was married I can say I was a virgin as far as Jesus Christ is concerned - in His eyes.

To those who have lost their virginity, I want to say, "It is something that can be gained back only through Jesus Christ. You can't gain it back through the world, or through anything else. Only through Jesus Christ can you gain back your virginity, and be pure in His eyes. The only thing that really matters is what the Lord says about you anyway."

Crystal: If you ask for forgiveness, Jesus wants to give you back your purity, and He is waiting to cleanse and purify you. But I am going to tell you there are major consequences for not waiting for marriage."

Do you have any last words?

Jeff: If anything needs to be dealt with, and taught, it is sexual purity and how to stay pure before marriage. Sexual impurity is the one thing that can wreck a relationship, and ruin a life.

Right now, I'm speaking from a man's point of view. There is so much stuff out there that seems innocent at first, but it can drag you down into the pits. It will seem like you'll never be able to get out.

Sexual impurity is very difficult to get out of. Why? There is so much access to it. Anyone can turn on a computer, type in a few words, and they are there. In this day and age it is so difficult, especially for men. We are visually tempted, whereas women are emotionally tempted.

I want to say this to young men, "As far as remaining sexually pure, hang out with friends you know who are going to help you remain accountable, and remain sexually pure. That was a major factor in helping me to stay pure with Crystal. We had struggles like anybody else."

Crystal: "Abstinence is the only safe and effective way to control your life. Putting aside all spiritual things, it is still the best thing to do. It is the best choice physically, and you won't get "soul ties."

I challenge you to find yourself, to see who you are. If you know who you are, you know you have value. You won't need to tell so and so,

"Sleep with me." You won't need to find that instant gratification."

You need to understand *who God is*, and *who you are in Jesus Christ.* You need to know that God loves you! Find out about God for yourself! Don't conjure up anything, and don't think it's always going to be emotional either.

I Corinthians 3:16 says our bodies are "...the temple of God." Start taking care of your body, and your life. Have pride in yourself.

Strive for diligence, excellence, character, and integrity.

Pursue purity and don't be conformed to the media, magazines, and what Hollywood is doing. Stop looking at media pop stars as your idol. Find a good mentor in your life that will speak the truth in love.

Remember, at the end of the day, when the sun sets, you only have to please one man who will love you unconditionally... God."

Following are excerpts from Dr. James Dobson's book *Preparing For Adolescence* which are relevant to our subject.

"This appetite for sex is something that God created within you. I want to make this point very strongly. Sex is not dirty, and it is not evil. Nothing that God created could be dirty.

The desire for sex was God's idea - not ours. He placed this part of our nature into us; He created those chemicals (hormones) that make the opposite sex so appealing to us. He did this so we would want to have a family of our own. Without this desire there would be no marriage, and no children, and no love between a man and a woman.

So, sex is not a dirty thing at all. It is a wonderful, beautiful mechanism, no matter what you may have heard about it. However, I must also tell you that God intends for us to control that desire for sexual intercourse.

He has stated repeatedly in the Bible that we are to save our body for the person we will

41

eventually marry, and that it is wrong to satisfy our appetite for sex with a boy or girl before we get married. There is just no other way to interpret the Biblical message.

Some of your friends may tell you differently in the days ahead. You may hear of Jack or Susie, Paul or Jane tell you about how they explored each others bodies. They'll tell you how exciting it was, and try to get you to do the same.

It is very likely that you will have a chance to have sexual intercourse before you reach twenty years of age. You will be with a person of the opposite sex who will let you know that he or she will permit you to have this experience.

You are going to have to decide between now and then what you'll do about that moment when it comes. You probably won't have time to think when it suddenly happens.

My strongest advice is for you to decide right now to save your body for the one who will eventually be your marriage partner.

If you don't control this desire, you will later wish that you had."

Preparing For Adolescence by Dr. James Dobson

CONCLUSION

I made a total mess of my life. Over and over again, I kept doing the wrong thing. My mom said, "Sondra, I tried to help you do the right thing, but you always headed in the wrong direction."

I did not walk in sexual purity. I was a Sunday morning Christian. I refused the love of God and others. I was an isolationist.

Rebellion and anger ruled my actions.

I knew I was doing wrong, but I chose my path away from God. I carry the scars of those actions within my soul.

Yet, God was still there ready to forgive and cleanse me... when... and if... I asked Him.

The purity I longed for, I found in God.

By surrendering my life to God, He restored everything. He gave me what I felt was unattainable... and that was pure love.

44

If you don't know God or His Son, Jesus, you can:

John 3:16 says, "For God so loved the world (that's you and me) that He gave His only begotten Son, that whosoever (that's you and me) believes in Him should not perish, but have everlasting life." KJV (italicized words inserted by author)

Romans 10:9, "For whosoever shall call upon the name of the Lord, shall be saved." KJV

Acts 4:12, "Neither is there salvation in any other, for there is none other name under heaven given among men, whereby we must be saved." KJV

You can pray a simple prayer: "Jesus, I repent of my sins. I ask You to come into my heart. I surrender my life to You. I make You my Lord and Savior."

If you prayed that prayer, I believe you have been saved, "born again." Please find a good, Bible-based church to attend. Keep God first place in your life.

God believes in you. I believe in you.

To contact the author write:

Sondra Largent
P.O. Box 680524
Orlando, Florida 32868

*Please include your prayer request and
comments when you write.*

NOTES

www.ingramcontent.com/pod-product-compliance
Lightning Source LLC
Chambersburg PA
CBHW060626030426
42337CB00018B/3210